ALL OF THE WILD

The Language of Chimpanzees and Other Primates

Megan Kopp

Cavendish
Square

New York

Published in 2017 by Cavendish Square Publishing, LLC
243 5th Avenue, Suite 136, New York, NY 10016

Website: cavendishsq.com

This publication represents the opinions and views of the author based on his or her personal experience, knowledge, and
research. The information in this book serves as a general guide only. The author and publisher have used their best efforts
in preparing this book and disclaim liability rising directly or indirectly from the use and application of this book.

CPSIA Compliance Information: Batch #CS16CSQ

All websites were available and accurate when this book was sent to press.

Library of Congress Cataloging-in-Publication Data

Names: Kopp, Megan, author.
Title: The language of Chimpanzees and other primates / Megan Kopp.
Description: New York : Cavendish Square Publishing, [2017] | Series: Call of the wild | Includes bibliographical references
and index. | Description based on print version record and CIP data provided by publisher; resource not viewed.
Identifiers: LCCN 2016000339 (print) | LCCN 2015051336 (ebook) | ISBN 9781502617156 (ebook) |
ISBN 9781502617279 (pbk.) | ISBN 9781502617217 (library bound) | ISBN 9781502617095 (6 pack)
Subjects: LCSH: Primates--Vocalization--Juvenile literature. | Primates--Behavior--Juvenile literature. | Animal
communication--Juvenile literature.
Classification: LCC QL737.P9 (print) | LCC QL737.P9 K65 2017 (ebook) | DDC 599.8159--dc23
LC record available at http://lccn.loc.gov/2016000339

Editorial Director: David McNamara
Editor: Kelly Spence
Copy Editor: Rebecca Rohan
Art Director: Jeffrey Talbot
Designer: Joseph Macri
Production Assistant: Karol Szymczuk
Photo Research: J8 Media

The photographs in this book are used by permission and through the courtesy of: Louise Murray/robertharding/Getty
Images, cover; Andrew Plumptre/Oxford Scientific/Getty Images, 4; Kate Capture/Shutterstock.com, 5; Jean Michel Labat/
Mary Evans Picture Library/AGE Fotostock, 6; David Seaford/Alamy Stock Photo, 7; Frans Lanting/Mint Images/Getty
Images, 8; Ian Nichols/National Geographic Magazines/Getty Images, 10; Fernando Sanchez Cortes/Shutterstock.com,
11; Ralph Lee Hopkins/National Geographic/Getty Images, 12; Anup Shah/Stone/Getty Images, 14; Rodney Brindamour/
National Geographic/Getty Images, 15; Suzi Eszterhas/Minden Pictures/Getty Images, 16; bimserd/Shutterstock.com, 18;
Danita Delimont/Gallo Images/Getty Images, 19; Ger Bosma/Moment Open/Getty Images, 20; Pete Oxford/Minden Pic-
tures/Getty Images, 23; namatae/Shutterstock.com, 24; ZUMA Press, Inc./Alamy Stock Photo, 26 (top); Kyodo/Newscom,
26 (bottom); Everett Collection Inc./Alamy Stock Photo, 27.

Printed in the United States of America

CONTENTS

Animal Communication

If you want to get someone's attention, you might call out. You might wave. You might even whistle. All of these actions are types of communication. Communication is the **exchange** of information between one individual and another.

TALKING WITHOUT WORDS

Unlike humans, animals do not use words to communicate. Instead, they use **signals** or displays. Many animals use sounds such as whistles and **hoots** to signal other animals. Others use touch. Animals also use body language to show their feelings and to send messages.

WHAT DO YOU MEAN?

Many animals live in groups. Imagine trying to get a group to do something when you can't send a signal. Try getting your friends to come over and play when you can't talk, wave, point, or send any **visual** or physical message.

Young orangutans learn by watching their parents.

Young animals use signals to recognize their parents. Parents receive signals from their young to find them in a group. Signals, such as sound, are used to help animals tell other animals where they are.

Animals exchange signals to show power. They also use signals to set up or guard their **territory**. Animals use sound, sight, and smell to say "this is my space." Signals are also used to find food and to let others know if there is danger ahead.

Chimpanzees have more than thirty different calls.

Howler monkeys use their loud calls to tell other groups that a territory is occupied.

ALL ABOUT PRIMATES

Primates include animals such as chimpanzees, monkeys, gorillas, and orangutans. Chimpanzees are humans' closest animal **relative**. They communicate in ways similar to ours. Let's find out more!

Bonobos, once called pygmy chimpanzees, groom one another to build and maintain social relationships.

CHAPTER ONE

Chatting about Chimpanzees

Chimpanzees live in groups. They are **social** animals. Communication is key to their success as a **species**.

TALK LIKE A CHIMPANZEE

Chimpanzees are vocal creatures. They make many different sounds. They grunt, bark, hoot, and whimper. Some of these calls can be heard as far away as 2 miles (3.2 kilometers). Chimps use calls to let other chimpanzees know where to find food. They grunt softly when resting in

Communication is necessary, rain or shine!

groups or looking for food. This helps keep the group together as they move through the forest.

They also have special calls to communicate about something that is unusual or dangerous. Each individual has a special hoot. This hoot is similar to a person's name. It is how chimpanzees identify each other.

THE SCIENCE BEHIND A CHIMP'S BRAIN

Humans are primates, just like chimpanzees. The difference is our brains. Humans have developed further than chimps. Chimpanzee brains grow quickly before birth. Human brains continue to grow after birth and over the first few years of life. A human brain is about three times larger than that of a chimpanzee.

BODY LANGUAGE

Chimpanzees use postures, **gestures**, and sounds to set up boundaries. If a chimpanzee is angry it will stand up, wave its arms, throw rocks, or scowl. When one wants to comfort another, they touch and kiss. Chimpanzees will also **groom** each other. This communicates friendship. These actions also send a calming message.

Touch is an important communication tool.

SPECIES STATS

Chimpanzees eat both plants and animals. They weigh from 70 to 130 pounds (32 to 60 kilograms). Chimps can stand up to 5.5 feet (1.7 meters) tall. They live in groups called communities. Chimpanzees are found in central Africa.

Orangutans spend most of their lives in trees.

CHAPTER TWO

Hanging Out with Orangutans

Orangutan means "person of the forest." Orangutans have many human-like methods of communication. Sight and sound are the most important senses used by these animals to send and receive messages.

CALL OF THE WILD AND NOT-SO-WILD!

Male orangutans can make very loud calls. These calls can last for up to one minute and be heard from miles away. They make these calls to let other males know

A young orangutan will spend six or seven years with its mother.

that this is their territory. Female orangutans use calls to encourage their young. Mothers also use sound to let their young know when they have done something wrong.

Orangutans make what is called a "kiss squeak" when alarmed. Scientists have noticed that some orangutans place a cupped hand or leaf in front of their mouths when making this sound. This makes the sound louder. If a **predator** is nearby, this louder call suggests that the orangutan is large. The predator may give up its hunt based on this information.

A captive orangutan in Germany has learned to make sounds like humans. Tilda clicks her tongue, whistles, and can make vowel sounds. She uses these sounds to get the attention of humans when she wants more food. Tilda also claps or points at food while she makes these noises.

ACTING OUT

Orangutans are known to act out ideas in order to communicate with humans and other apes. It is like a game of **charades**. Orangutans

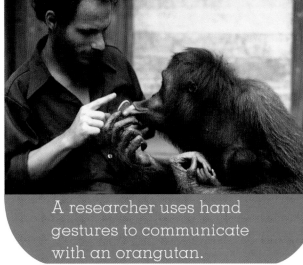

A researcher uses hand gestures to communicate with an orangutan.

can act out ideas with body movements to send a message. In one case, a female orangutan acted out a scene where a human had helped heal her hurt foot. Another orangutan pretended that she couldn't open a coconut with a stick. She handed the coconut to a human and pretended to use the stick like a big knife. The researcher cut the coconut open and the orangutan was happy.

SPECIES STATS

Orangutans live only in Sumatra and Borneo. They can weigh up to 180 pounds (82 kg) and stand 5 feet (1.5 m) tall. Orangutans eat mostly fruit and leaves. Orangutans are loners and do not live in groups.

A warm hug communicates safety to these young mountain gorillas.

CHAPTER THREE

Greeting Mountain Gorillas

M ountain gorillas are social animals. Sound, smell, and sight are important senses used by mountain gorillas to communicate within the group.

GORILLA GRUNTS

More than just grunts, gorillas use at least twenty-two different sounds to communicate. They range from an adult male's roar of anger to an infant's whimper for its mother. Mountain gorillas take a nap in the middle of the day. Grunts are used to announce when it's time to get up.

The silverback protects and makes decisions for the entire group.

SOMETHING SMELLS

Adult males are called silverbacks. Silverbacks sometimes let off a strong smell to keep predators away. It's a smelly way to say, "We don't taste good, so go find other food." Mountain gorillas also communicate through other scents. These smells are filled with information. The scents share details about a gorilla's health, age, and whether they are male or female.

THE LOOK ON YOUR FACE

Gorillas have expressive faces. A gorilla can look unfriendly with a fixed gaze and its lips pressed together. They can look scared with shifting eyes and an open mouth, showing their teeth. Gorillas show they want to play with an open mouth but no teeth showing. Gorillas do not like being stared at. It shows **aggression**.

One shocked gorilla!

SPECIES STATS

Bands or troops of mountain gorillas can be found living on mountain slopes in central Africa. Mountain gorillas eat plant leaves, shoots, and stems. They also eat fruit, ants, snails, and **grubs**. An adult male gorilla can eat more than 40 pounds (18 kg) of food in a single day.

Several howler monkeys join in a loud chorus.

CHAPTER FOUR

Howling with Howler Monkeys

Their name says it all: howler monkeys howl! These primates are loud and vocal. There is no mistaking their presence in the rain forest.

CALLING OUT LOUD

Howler monkeys have two types of loud calls. Barks are short and harsh. They are used for getting attention. Roars are deep and loud. Males will start the roaring, but all of the monkeys can join in.

These calls can be heard up to 3 miles (5 km) away. Most roaring is done in the morning or evening. It is a way to mark territory so others stay away. These calls also communicate group location and makeup.

THE STARE DOWN AND OTHER SIGNALS

Howler monkeys are very social animals. Because they live in large groups, communication is important to help them get along. Howler monkeys have expressive faces. They use body movements to get their messages across. Staring is a threat. Grinning, head bobbing, and yawning are all signs of anger. Grooming is a way to make peace or show

Black howler monkeys are one of the ten different species of howler monkeys.

affection. Howler monkeys also communicate within their group by blinking, waggling their tongues, and making clicking sounds.

THE SCIENCE BEHIND A HOWLER MONKEY'S CALL

A howler monkey's call is strengthened by a large, cup-shaped bone located in its throat. This hollow bone, called the **hyoid**, vibrates and turns up the sound when they call. Males have larger hyoid bones than females.

A young chimpanzee begs for food.

CHAPTER FIVE

Communicating with Primates

Humans are fascinated with primates. Many of the ways they share information are similar to ours. Some primates shake their head "no" to stop their young from doing something wrong. Others beg for food with an open hand. Gorillas, chimpanzees, and young orangutans show joy by laughing when they are tickled.

TALKING APE

It's no wonder that scientists continue to look for other ways to connect with primates. Monkeys and gorillas do not speak with words like humans. But that does not mean they can't communicate. A gorilla named Koko was taught to share messages using **sign language**.

A pair of twin orangutans living at the Miami Zoo use iPads to communicate. The special software they use was designed for humans with **autism**. It uses pictures of different objects. A trainer names an object and the orangutan presses the picture that matches. The apes use the iPads to draw, play games, and build their **vocabularies**.

Like many six-year-olds, Budi the orangutan enjoys playing with an iPad.

IN THE FIELD

Jane Goodall was fascinated by animals as a child. In 1960, she moved to the African forests of Tanzania to study chimpanzees. At first, she watched the animals from far away with binoculars. Over time, she was able to interact with them. Goodall was the first researcher to see a chimpanzee make and use a tool. Scientists believed that humans were the only species that made and used tools. Goodall proved them wrong. She is a leading scientist in chimpanzee intelligence and communication.

Glossary

aggression A hostile or violent behavior or attitude toward another.

autism A condition that causes someone to have trouble communicating.

charades A game in which players guess a word or phrase from clues told by gestures and facial expressions rather than words.

exchange To give and receive.

gestures Movements of parts of the body in order to communicate a feeling or an intention.

groom To take care of appearance and cleanliness.

grubs The wormlike young of some insects.

hoots To make sounds like an owl.

hyoid A horseshoe-shaped bone located in the throat of many mammals.

predator An animal that survives by hunting other animals for food.

primates Members of the group of mammals that includes monkeys and apes.

relative Connected to something else.

signals Sounds or actions used to send messages or warnings.

sign language A language in which hand gestures, in combination with facial expressions and larger body movements, are used instead of speech.

social Living in groups rather than as individuals.

species One of the groups into which similar animals are divided.

territory Any large area of land.

visual Of or having to do with seeing.

vocabularies Words used in languages.

Find Out More

Books

Franchino, Vicky. *Gorillas*. Nature's Children. New York: Scholastic, 2013.

Goldner, Rita. *Orangutan: A Day in the Rainforest Canopy*. Sedona, AZ: Dancing Dakini Press, 2015.

Shaffer, Jody Jensen. *Chimpanzees*. The Smartest Animals. Edina, MN: Abdo Publishing, 2014.

Websites

National Geographic: Gorilla Talk

video.nationalgeographic.com/video/exploreorg/gorilla-talk-eorg

Watch gorillas communicate in the wild.

National Geographic Kids: Chimpanzees

kids.nationalgeographic.com/animals/chimpanzee/#chimpanzeewithbaby.jpg

Discover the world of chimpanzees.

Index

About the Author

Megan Kopp is a freelance writer whose passions include science, nature, and the outdoors. She is the author of close to sixty titles for young readers. She loves research and has even gone so far as volunteering to be rescued from a snow cave to get a story about training avalanche rescue dogs. Kopp lives in the foothills of the Canadian Rocky Mountains, where she spends her spare time hiking, camping, and canoeing. One of her dreams is to hike in Rwanda to see mountain gorillas.